Magic Animals

GWENDOLYN MacEWEN

MAGIC ANIMALS

SELECTED POEMS OLD AND NEW

Macmillan of Canada   Toronto

I would like to express my gratitude to the editors
of the many Canadian magazines in which most of
these poems first appeared, to the publishers of
THE RISING FIRE, to the publishers of A BREAK-
FAST FOR BARBARIANS, to the C.B.C. for
numerous broadcasts of some of these poems,
and once again, to the Canada Council, for the
financial assistance which enabled me to complete
this book. Certain poems from SELAH and THE
DRUNKEN CLOCK, my first, privately-printed col-
lections, appear now in a revised form, as do some
of the selections from THE RISING FIRE.

ISBN 0-7705-1214-3 cloth
ISBN 0-7705-1206-2 paper

Printed in Canada
for The Macmillan Company of Canada Limited
70 Bond Street, Toronto M5B 1X3

For Nikos, who makes it all possible

Table of Contents

Part One: Selected Poems, 1961-1972

Part Two: Magic Animals, 1972-1974

Part One: Selected Poems, 1961-1972

Icarus

Feather and wax, the artful wings
bridge a blue gulf between
the stiff stone tower
and its languid god, fat sky.

The boy, bent to the whim of wind,
the blue, and the snarling sun
form a brief triumvirate
—flesh, feather, light—
locked in the jaws of the noon
they rule with fleeting liberty.

> These are the wings, then,
> a legacy of hollow light—
> feathers, a quill to write
> white poetry across the sky.

Through the mouth of the air, the boy
sees his far father, whose muscled flight
is somehow severed from his own.
Two blinking worlds, and Daedalus'
unbound self is a thing apart.

> You, bound for that other area
> know that this legacy of mindflight
> is all you have to leave me.

The boy, Icarus, twists the threads of his throat
and his eyes argue with the sun
on a flimsy parallel, and
the mouth of the sun eager, eager,
smuggles a hot word to the boy's ear.

> But flying, locked in dark dream,
> I see Queen Dream, Queen Flight,
> the last station of the poet
> years above my brow, and

Something, something in the air,
in the light's flight, in the vaguely
voluptuous arc of the wings
drives a foreign rhythm into his arms,
his arms which are lean, white willows.

Icarus feels his blood race to his wrist
in a marathon of red light. Swifter,
swift, he tears away the slow veil
from his tendons; the playful biceps
sing; they wish new power to the beautiful
false wings
and the boy loops up into tall cobalt.
His hair is a swirl of drunken light,
his arms are wet blades; wings wed with arms.

                You knew
                I would get drunk on beauty.
                The famous phantom quill
                would write me, pull me
                through the eye
                of needle noon.

Crete is a huge hump of a black whore beneath him.
Her breasts, two wretched mountains
tremble under his eye.
All is black, except the sun in slow explosion;
a great war strangles his vision
and knots his flying nerve.
Black, and fire, and the boy.

                You and your legacy!
                You knew I would try to
                slay the sunlight.

Look, Icarus has kissed the sun
and it sucks the wax,

feathers and wax.
The wings are melting!

The boy Icarus is lean and beautiful.
His body grows limp and falls.
It is cruel poetry set
to the tempo of lightning; it is too swift,
this thin descent.

On the lips of the Aegean:
globules of wax,
strands of wet light,

     the lean poem's flesh
     tattered and torn
     by a hook
     of vengeful fire . . .

Combustion of brief feathers

Eden, Eden

the thunder is
a vocal monument
to the dying rain
or an obelisk in a granite sky
which roars an epitaph
through cut clouds.

in the morning
thunder is a reared stone elephant,
                      a grown element of grey;
its trunk is vertical and thick as—thunder;
it roars down the wrenched lightning
coughing out a verse
for the suicidal rain
in the morning.

the stormed man is heavy with rain
and mumbles beneath the elephant's gargle
and his jaws lock human in the rain,
and under the unlocked jaws of the split sky
and under the bullets of the elephant's trunk

he is thinking of a thunder garden.

behind sense he is thinking of a warped tree
with heavy fruit falling,
peaked rock fighting the ragged fern
in *another* storm-centre —
a monolithic thunder tree
and a man and woman naked and green with rain
above its carved roots, genesis

The Drunken Clock

The bells ring more than Sunday; Eve,
orchards and high wishes meet the bells
with grace and speed. The staggered
clocks only cousin the bells; after
the timed food, the urgent breakfasts,
we lean to other seasons, seasons

of the first temple
of a basic Babel
of Sumer
of meek amoeba

Clocks count forward with craze, but
bells count backward with sober grace.
Tell us, in the high minute after they
sing, where the temple is, where
the bell's beat breaks all our hourglass, where the jungled flesh
is tied, bloodroots

The Breakfast

under the knuckles of the warlord sun how long do we have
how long do we have, you ask, in the vast magenta wastes
of the morning world when the bone buckles under for war
when the bone intersects as tangent in the district of the sun
centipedes and infidels; snakes and the absence of doves?

a breakfast hysteria; perhaps you have felt it,
the weight of the food you eat, the end of the meal coming
before you lift the spoon; or eat only apples
to improvise an eden, or forget the end takes place
in each step of your function.

look, the spoon is lifted halfway through invisible tables
of dangerous logarithms in the abstract morning spaces;
come, come—eat leviathans in the breakfast wastelands,
eat bestiaries and marine zoos and apples and aviaries.
by eating the world you may enclose it.

seek simplicities; the fingerprints of the sun only
and the fingernails of the moon duplicating you in your body.
the cosmos meets your measures, has no ending.

place one hand before the sun and make it smaller,
hold the spoon in your hand up to the sky
and marvel at its relative size; comfort yourself
with the dimensions of a momentary breakfast table.

ah lord sun
ah terrible atomic breakfast
ah twilight of purple fallout
ah last deck of evening cards—

deal, infidel, the night is indeed difficult

Tiamut

A woman called Chaos, she
was the earth inebriate, without form,
a thing of ripped green flesh
and forests in crooked wooden dance
and water a wine drunk on itself
and boulders bumping into foolish clouds.

Tiamut, her breasts in mountainous collision,
her womb a cave of primeval beasts, her thighs torn
greatly in the black Babylonian pre-eden

winced at the coming of Marduk;
his hands laid her flat and angry on a bed of void;
Marduk stretched her out, and she lay there
coughing up black phlegm.

Marduk flattened her belly under one hand
and sliced Tiamut down the length of her body
(the argument of parts, the division of disorder)
and made the sky from her left side
and fashioned the earth from her right.

We, caught on a split organ of chaos,
on the right half of a bisected goddess,
wonder why the moon pulls the sea on a silver string,
why the earth will not leave the gold bondage of the sun,
why all parts marry, all things couple in confusion
while atoms are wrenched apart in this
adolescent time.

Universe And

something we know of mountains
and craters within craters—
big braille under a blind God's hands

      space. our timorous temples turn
      inward, our introverted temples
      turn, as the flyer hoists our vision
      higher

on earth, the machines of our myth
grind down, grind slowly now, rusting
the wheels of human sense

      we drink white milk while
      high galactic fields open
      their floodgates   open

and the terrible laughter of our children
is heard in that pocket, that
high white place above our thunder

Universe And: The Electric Garden

the protons and the neutrons move, gardener,
sire their suns, spirals of sense,
and servant their planets,
their negative pebbles
in a pool of moons; electrons like
mad bees
        circle;
            the nuclei reach out
to harness them;
            will of the sun reaches out,
straps earth, straps moon, slowly excites
other stars, sets, sets the sweet fanatic pace
going;
            telescopes turn inward, bend down.

in our gardens are electric roses
which spark, push light, push fuchsia
through flailing grass

and spines of long magnetic seas cloy,
rake their depths for dust; all holds;
the spines hold the elemental jelly
of the sea's flesh there.

I walk warily through
my electric garden.

Nikolayev and Popovich: The Cosmic Brothers

all orbits complement
the logic we derive
from eggshell symmetry
of satellites or sweet
concentric circles
of crumbs and insects
on cosmic tablecloths;
we have no dimensions, and
the burden of thinking
in terms of size
is lifted from us;
make no discrepancy
between the cosmic egg
and the eye's diameter.

the fact that there are two
is not the thing,
beyond the sense that brothers spring
from a common womb, and naturally
if the oval orbit claims the one,
earth's green uterus might
reclaim the other.

but look to limits for a minute
as the inverted eye looks inward
to find the inner eye looking out
as finally, the astronauts swim
through the yellow yolks of total suns
towards the ultimate inquiry—
(even the darkness has
a certain intelligence)—
and find at the end of the universe
not walls, but mirrors
reflecting the question mark
of their own faces back in,
to study it ironically,
like brothers, amazed
at their own similarity.

The Room of the Last Supper: Mount Zion

we flock clicking cameras quickly
for the Enemy is watching us; gnomes,
we substitute lenses for eyes between the pillars
as though the burrowing film
will register later
the Feast in negative, or
we have gouged out darkness
and now we too are hungry and
hunt for crumbs amid the whiteness.

The Dimensions of a Tiger

the cat in the grass lengthens—
and your tendons reach widely
into seasons of wind and deltas—
you are suddenly aware that
you have no boundaries, that
you are a field with no fences.

hollyhock and frolic, you
are the width of wind and voices
until something, a microscopic irony
like laughter breaking from windows
or a diminutive rain shrinks you
and the cat in the grass curls under.

The Phoenix

beyond you, the image rising from your shoulders
is greater than you, as the phoenix from the fire
is risen, as the rising fire on the opening wings
is greater than the stirring and potential pyre.

you appear in the weekdays of your wishes
or in musical Sundays and make on an instrument's strings
idly, high harmonics which transcend the note
and will not believe that these are also wings.

enter and re-enter the burning of your city
in the heat of the weekday, with anything enter
innocently lyric, with gravity, or phallic,
you who are beautiful and difficult to suffer.

observe that your anatomy is fire and brains are ashes
and in the terms of old madness, sleep with queens;
take root; the most available loins are here
to place the equivocal seeds between.

circuses of knees, and the bone trapezes
out from its first wish to the bone of another—
past the most pleasant of all anatomies
where one trapeze succeeds the other—

or start to fly and inevitably the phoenix
flies parallel to you, nibbling idly on your brain,
lost for its nest of innocent ash, the weekdays
of its sleeping, terrified of its own fire again.

God how we doubt the flames of our beauty!
now grow in the burning and demanding city
seeds of our excellence, reasons for phoenixes,
rake ash from our bodies for a new anatomy!

—take you fighting from the weekdays of your vision
—from the city burning in terms of old madness

23

—past your shoulders to the image beyond them
—past the note to the high harmonic
—from the comfortable ash-nest of the brain's old reason
—to the constant Sunday where the fires keep rising.

For Alick MacEwen: d. 1960

what we have left behind us in the fathering clay,
the finishing bed where the veins flow grey
in the grave unequivocal, is little, redundancy.

long long beneath the morning moon of our halfway
vision, our wrong repent repeats, stalls
the noon coming, is wrong recalling.

(stolen, stolen by the thieves of gravity,
the inverse womb, the inward worm, etc.
O God forgive us these, etc.)

but say you chase life the way you chase
the sunset in grey jets on sunday still
though an organist's veins are opening

for the last warm music; you
were classic somewhere in Canada on sunday
touching trees where old apples fall and birds occur —

(give us that particular cruelty necessary
to take it, your life, a second time, it is
time to speak the truth, it is time to speak,
it is time)

The Pied Piper

was he only
I ask you
a magnet, radical
and yellow in their towns
or a gay science, I ask
you, was he only
momentary messiah, was
he only these?

children still wait
for the absurd
red and yellow music; they
have not forgotten
him tho you wish
they would

forget, always forget
the piper, the pied
piper, the red and yellow
piper. O gentlemen,
in your cities of rats
someone hears a gentle music,
someone laughs.

Generation Cometh

the boy
a coy root or
bright among cities
is growing, you
cannot stop him, you
cannot stop him
growing.

try to
pull him out
by the roots
from your loins, he
is green like a tree
planted there.

he is in your dark garden
he will eat your dark flowers
you cannot stop him, old
men, old women, you
cannot stop him
growing.

his thumb, his
bright brain, his
heel is beneath you;
send him to school
or macabre churches, you
cannot stop him
growing.

not even the wild
Muria boy stood
wild and white-toothed
among jungles
and found them
complicated.

he grows beneath your heels
and the city for him is easy, he
knows it from below;
old men, old women, you
cannot stop him
growing.

A Breakfast For Barbarians

my friends, my sweet barbarians,
there is that hunger which is not for food—
but an eye at the navel turns the appetite
round
with visions of some fabulous sandwich,
the brain's golden breakfast
                              eaten with beasts
                              with books on plates

let us make an anthology of recipes,
let us edit for breakfast
our most unspeakable appetites—
let us pool spoons, knives
and all cutlery in a cosmic cuisine,
let us answer hunger
with boiled chimera
and apocalyptic tea,
an arcane salad of spiced bibles,
tossed dictionaries—
                    (O my barbarians
                    we will consume our mysteries)

and can we, can we slake the gaping eye of our desires?
we will sit around our hewn wood table
until our hair is long and our eyes are feeble,
eating, my people, O my insatiates,
eating until we are no more able
to jack up the jaws any longer—

to no more complain of the soul's vulgar cavities,
to gaze at each other over the rust-heap of cutlery,
drinking a coffee that takes an eternity—
till, bursting, bleary,
we laugh, barbarians, and rock the universe—
and exclaim to each other over the table
over the table of bones and scrap metal
over the gigantic junk-heaped table:

by God that was a meal

The Garden of Square Roots: An Autobiography

and then the rattlesnake spines of men distracted me
for even they, the people were
as Natajara was, who danced
while I was anchored like a passive verb
or Neptune on a subway—

and from the incredible animal i
grew queer claws inward to fierce cribs;
I searched gardens for square roots,
for i was the I interior
the thing with a gold belt and delicate ears
with no knees or elbows
was working from the inside out

this city I live in I built with bones
and mortared with marrow;
I planned it in my spare time
and its hydro is charged from a blood niagara
and I built this city backwards and
the people evolved out of the buildings
and the subway uterus ejected them—

for i was the I interior
the thing with a gold belt and delicate ears
with no knees or elbows
was working from the inside out.

and all my gardens grew backwards
and all the roots were finally square
and Ah! the flowers grew there like algebra

Poems in Braille

1
all your hands are verbs,
now you touch worlds and feel their names—
thru the thing to the name
not the other way thru (in winter
I am Midas, I name gold)

the chair and table and book
extend from your fingers;
all your movements
command these things back to their
places; a fight against familiarity
makes me resume my distance

2
they knew what it meant,
those egyptian scribes who drew
eyes right into their hieroglyphs,
you read them dispassionate until
the eye stumbles upon itself
blinking back from the papyrus

outside, the articulate wind
annotates this; I read carefully
lest I go blind in both eyes, reading with
that other eye the final hieroglyph

3
the shortest distance between 2 points
on a revolving circumference
is a curved line; O let me follow you,
Wenceslas

4
with legs and arms I make alphabets
like in those children's books
where people bend into letters and signs,

yet I do not read the long cabbala of my bones
truthfully; I need only to move
to alter the design

5
I name all things in my room
and they rehearse their names,
gather in groups, form tesseracts,
discussing their names among themselves

I will not say the cast is less than the print
I will not say the curve is longer than the line,
I should read all things like braille in this season
with my fingers I should read them
lest I go blind in both eyes reading with
that other eye the final hieroglyph

Strange Breakfasts

I have eaten
strange breakfasts
with you.

Insatiate. These breakfasts
have broken the past
of smashed appetites;
that colossal intake
of morning images
has made me insatiate (ah you
and your coloured hungers
who doth enclose my life and my death
in your coffee—friend,
we cannot live too long)

obviously we are preparing for some final feast,
obviously our bellies stretch
for a supreme reason, obviously
we can stomach anything now, anything.

that these breakfasts have broken the past
hungers, hungers that were controlled,
controlled hungers, that these breakfasts
have broken them, that everyone does not wish
executed fish and fried eggs,
that the full belly means only
a further hunger, that we cannot now return
to younger appetites, that we can no longer
eat the bright ancestral food,
that we alone must set all our tables single-handed,
that we alone must account for the grease of our spoons
that we alone must wash our mouths
that we alone must look back and decline
all dinner offers,
that we alone will walk into the city at 9 o'clock
knowing that the others have also eaten
knowing that there is no time to compare the contents

of our bodies in our cities
that we eat and we eat and we know and we know
that machines work faster than the machines of our mouths

is why our breakfasts
get stranger and stranger.

Wombs: Some Thoughts and Observations

1

She had this little red bean with 10 ivory animals in it
carved in India. "Isn't it marvellous, Gwen," she said,
"10 ivory elephants inside this little red bean?"

and the bean was like, you know what, yes, like a womb,
that's what I said, a womb with 10 ivory elephants in it,
and I thought I wouldn't mind 10 ivory elephants
in mine, if it came down to that, I wouldn't mind it at all,
I'd enjoy it in fact—

now I've become rather over-selective,
I seek the lover who can accomplish this exacting act.

2

Salome the Immortal has a lab in Argentina
where she seeks to free women from the tyranny of the
    Moon,
yet I fear that all this Menstrual Research is a front,
for men are seen to enter Salome's private room. Besides,
they come and go in cycles, like eternal tides.

She

kallikrates recurs in black distances,
love is a frozen sundial, the shadows
freeze; the sex of her lover
drives through time like a solar thing
and Ayesha's body is a frozen flame—
Hes, who believes the cave where she sings
or the black ankh of the mountain above her,
its loop like a smoky womb—
Isis, who is aware of these things?

kallikrates kisses her in black distances,
love is a frozen sundial, the shadows
freeze; mouths like these shame time,
caves of cold flame await him—
now solid light enters the black loop of the ankh,
its shaft is held forever by Her;
Hes, I do not believe your song,
yet who is it waits for kallikrates to recur?

The Fire Dog

the cockle woman cries alive alive-o
in Poplar where the war is over, where
someone told me there are no poplars
she slurs the thrilled streets crying this
(and they are not alive, some of them
are dead, but she is only
talking about cockles)
meanwhile the poplar kids repeat
repeat it (alive alive-o) all daylong
and follow her with their faces cocked.
I mean War, of course. The Red Dog of Mars.
The Fire Dog.

someone told me the cockneys were good
at it (guts), like during the bombing
they stood in a hall
and in the silence before the bombs fell
one old guy screams HEY ANYONE WANNA BUY
A GOLD WATCH?
that kind of thing.

the children out of the loins of war
the children out of the loins of the fire dog
the children who follow the cockle woman
will build Rome out of their plasticine
will sit like catatonics with their statement of silence
will haunt us like small royal ghosts
will trample us with a clean fierce love

meanwhile, one cockle woman, one fire dog,
one bomb, one cockney in a hall HEY ANYONE
WANNA BUY A GOLD WATCH?

        alive
        alive
         o

The Children Are Laughing

It is monday and the children are laughing
The children are laughing; they believe they are princes
They wear no shoes; they believe they are princes
And their filthy kingdom heaves up behind them

The filthy city heaves up behind them
They are older than I am, their feet are shoeless
They have lived a thousand years; the children are laughing
The children are laughing and their death is upon them

I have cried in the city (the children are laughing)
I have worn many colours (the children are laughing)
They are older than I am, their death is upon them
I will wear no shoes when the princes are dying

The Metallic Anatomy

Civilization means that I am hardened at the knees
Yet welded delicate—my mind a sickle, a crescent tool
    Strikes a shrill metallic key—
Some days I am simply a long scream
    Sculptured in metal, incredible.

Some tensile art, precise with joy
Breaks my lines, keens me
    To a tense and resonant thing,
And the vats of boiling gold in my brain
    Harden to shrill and intricate shapes.

Now I tell you Fall on your knees
    Before the quivering girders of your city,
Fall on your beautiful precise knees
    Beneath me in the black streets;
This is not poetry, but clean greed—

There is a sculpture which must be made.
O citizen pose for this image of the city.

Poem Improvised Around a First Line*

the smoke in my bedroom which is always burning
worsens you, motorcycle Icarus;
you are black and leathery and lean and
you cannot distinguish between sex and nicotine

anytime, it's all one thing for you—
cigarette, phallus, sacrificial fire—
all part of that grimy flight
on wings axlegreased from Toronto to Buffalo
for the secret beer over the border—

now I long to see you fullblown and black
over Niagara, your bike burning and in full flame
and twisting and pivoting over Niagara
and falling finally into Niagara,
and tourists coming to see your black leather wings
hiss and swirl in the steaming current—

now I long to give up cigarettes
and change the sheets on my carboniferous bed;
O baby, what Hell to be Greek in this country—
without wings, but burning anyway

*The first line around which it was improvised has disappeared.

40

The Astronauts

now his orbit exceeds three,
exceeds me, my narrow turning,
his body has become a zodiac of bone,
its own myth, a personal cosmology—

I would say he orbits himself only,
his own body,
making his flesh supreme
within its sensual belts—
(but I know there is more than this
I know there is more,
nor can dwindle down those outward galaxies
to internal atoms anymore)

now, Yuri, your orbits
stress my gravity,
the kinetics of your flesh
escapes these lines,
(and you, Valentina, Russian Valentine,
female, dialectical, I imagine you
pivoting over the polar caps,
ferris-wheel woman, queen of hemispheres,
moving through the complex vacuum of a dream)

you flyers, where you are,
God does not need to be,
you have gashed the white void of His memory,
and orbits of verbs describe strange poetries—

I would kneel down under them, those orbits,
those huge and humming wheels,
while rockets rehearse a countdown
in the graded spaces of the spine,
then launched, arise to puncture
the positive zeros of the cosmos and the mind.

The Self Assumes

not love, lean and frequent,
but the accurate earth,
a naked landscape, green
yet free of seasons
is a name the violate self assumes
after its violent beginnings

not this complex dance of fire and blood
which burns the night to morning,
these hypnotic feet which turn us
know no end and no returning

but a fish within a brilliant river
whose body separates the dreaming waters
and never touches land
is a name the violate self assumes
as silver winds instruct the swimmer
who swims with neither feet nor hands

O not this double dance which burns the night to morning
and cracks the latitudes of time and sleep
whose lean and frequent fires in their burning
break apart the landscapes of a dream,
but the accurate self which burns, and burning, assumes
   green.

Tabgha: Church of Loaves and Fishes

the christian fish   is jigsaw
the piecemeal   byzantine art
is jigsaw. wait   the cock crows

blessed are
blessed are
blessed are

the footprints   of messiah are
mosaic   wait.   the cock crows

blessed are
blessed are
blessed are

there's something here   we must remember
something jigsaw

blessed are
blessed are
blessed are

blessed is the baked arab   the businessman
running a place called   Holyland Buffet
beside the mountain   of beatitudes
removed, secluded   absolutely objective
who would not blink   an eyelid if
christ came ordering beer   or
the cock   stopped   crowing

ISRAEL 1962

43

The Left Hand and Hiroshima

asked once why I fanned my fingers before my eyes
to screen the strange scream of them, I, sinister, replied:
Recently I dropped a bomb upon Hiroshima.

as for the mad dialectics of my tooth-chewed hands
I knew nothing; the left one was responsible and
abominably strong, bombed the flower of Hiroshima.

only because my poems are lies do they earn the right
to be true, like the lie of that left hand at night
in the cockpit of a sad plane trailing God in its wake.

all the left hands of your bodies, your loud thumbs
did accomplice me! men women children at the proud womb,
we have accomplished Hell. Woe Hiroshima . . .

you have the jekyll hand you have the hyde hand
my people, and you are abominable; but now I am proud and
in uttering love I occur four-fingered and garbed
in a broken gardener's glove over the barbed
                    garden
                    of Hiroshima . . .

Green With Sleep

Green with sleep the skin breathes night
—I hear you turning worlds in your dark dream—
The sheets like leaves in a private season
Speak of the singular self which lies between.

Your breathing is a thing I cannot enter
Like a season more remote than winter;
Green with sleep breathes, breathes the skin,
I hear you turning worlds in your dark dream.

There is a great unspeakable wheel which keeps
Us slender as myths, and green with sleep.

The Bead Spectrum

you laugh you cry you wear bright beads
and the colours love you, dozens
huddle upon you.

O lady, the world will not confess your colours
and nowhere are your beads acknowledged
against the spectrum of your city.

but your beads love you
and form their own spectrum
and your fingers fumble them
(infra-red to your throat's final violet)
as colours clash
and all the world's unspeakable accessories
shake like a stripper's machines
and its large horny music
exits you to nakedness.

now in your plural world
your colours huddle, confess themselves
upon your flesh (a pallid apocalypse) —
dynamos crash, and in your room sewing,
you laugh you cry you wear bright beads.

Do You Have the Time

maybe we could determine it by advanced calculus
now that our watches are broken
or by resorting to complicated instruments
now that our clocks are broken
or by making clepsydras and sundials
to pour time, shave time, save time
in the steel city, in its sunday streets
whose neutral pavements rush up to meet
the falling bodies of gods and clockmakers
in the morning, before church.

especially on sundays I want to hark
back to the mad instant preceding me,
for I too, no doubt, am an accident
of timing, like a million others
(whole continents are populated by
errors of calendars and clocks)—
yet still they give children
watches on their birthdays,
and they consult their own small wrists
to find out where they stand
(do you have the time? O how
can we tell, who live despite it?
Besides, we buried our watches in the sand)

The Last Breakfast

sometimes the food refuses to be sanctified
and you stand over the table beating your chest
and screaming impotent graces for bacon and eggs
graphic on the plate, arranged in a greasy cipher

aware that your body like a graceful vegetable
refuses to be holy; you stop screaming
grace for the eggs and the unsacred bacon,
you stop screaming and sit down darkly

hypnotized by two fried yellow eggs, by this
altogether kanadian breakfast, realizing
your appetite is jaded and the plate is blue
and the food has become an anathema

the bacon has nothing to say for itself
the whole thing is decidedly insane
but you eat the breakfast because it is there
to be eaten, and as you eat
you delicate barbarian, you think of pigs and chickens,
you think of mammoths and their tons of frozen ancient meat,
you think of dark men running through the earth
on their naked, splendid feet

Manzini: Escape Artist

now there are no bonds except the flesh; listen—
there was this boy, Manzini, stubborn with
gut stood with black tights and a turquoise
leaf across his sex

and smirking while the big
brute tied his neck arms legs, Manzini
naked waist up and white with sweat

struggled. Silent, delinquent, he
was suddenly all teeth and knee, straining slack
and excellent with sweat, inwardly

wondering if Houdini would take as long
as he; fighting time and the drenched
muscular ropes, as though his tendons were worn
on the outside—

as though his own guts were the ropes
encircling him; it was beautiful; it was thursday; listen—
there was this boy, Manzini

finally free, slid as snake from
his own sweet agonized skin, to throw his entrails
white upon the floor
with a cry of victory—

now there are no bonds except the flesh,
but listen, it was thursday, there was this boy,
Manzini—

49

Black Alchemy

Out of blackness and forth from black water
he moves, baptized at midnight
in the mercurial lake
whose waves transmuted him
from the hot metallic laughter

Of their wake. He is neither metal nor water
nor fluid nor solid, but born from the darkest
paradox of his body are forms without terms
and substances which seek their names in laughter.

Out of blackness, from a midnight alchemy
he moves, an accident, the second adam,
angry with birth, its brilliant disaster
defies him. The bones and the body harden.

Now he is a dervish, the prince of laughter
and the lake falls back from his tireless turning;
the burning ache of his black and brilliant body
cancels the cosmos, and in his dance

Worlds expire like tides, in his flaming
dance the nameless cosmos
must await his naming.

The Thing Is Violent

Self, I want you now to be
violent and without history,
for we've rehearsed too long our ceremonial ballet
and I fear my calm against your exquisite rage.

I do not fear that I will go mad
but that I may not, and the shadows of my sanity
blacken out your burning; act once
and you need not act again—
give me no ceremony, scars are not pain.

The thing is violent, nothing precedes it,
it has no meaning before or after—
sweet wounds which burn like stars,
stigmata of the self's own holiness,
appear and plot new zodiacs upon the flesh.

Appendectomy

it's interesting how you can brag about a scar;
I'm fascinated with mine; it's diagonal and straight,
it suggests great skill, great speed,
it is no longer or shorter than it needs to be.

it is good how it follows my natural symmetry
parallel to the hip, a perfect geometry;
it is not a wound; it is a diagram
drawn correctly, it has no connection with pain.

it's interesting how you can brag about a scar;
nothing in nature is a straight line
except this delightful blasphemy on my belly;
the surgeon was an Indian, and beautiful, and holy.

The Caravan

precede me into this elusive country,
travel the tracks of my old laughter,
tame this landscape, and I will follow after—
yet do not let this desert inherit you,
absorb your caravan into sand—
(which is your body, which is the land?)
O love elude me, this recurring journey
darkens my speech, disorients me
forever from my natural country,
while the orient eye decides geography.

bandar abbes, el minya, el gatrun,
taif, dongola, beni abbes . . .
(once, during an eclipse
the polarities of my body argued me out
from an arctic dream
and I journeyed east, and south,
to enter the final africa of your mouth)

my caravan falters, stops and starts,
its tracks upon the sand are arabesque;
this night is a dream of jackals
and disorient, I cannot decide which turn is best,
and so I circle, so I dance—
(precede me into this elusive country)
always this place, this latitude escapes me

The Red Bird You Wait For

You are waiting for someone to confirm it,
You are waiting for someone to say it plain,
Now we are here and because we are short of time
I will say it; I might even speak its name.

It is moving above me, it is burning my heart out,
I have felt it crash through my flesh,
I have spoken to it in a foreign tongue,
I have stroked its neck in the night like a wish.

Its name is the name you have buried in your blood,
Its shape is a gorgeous cast-off velvet cape,
Its eyes are the eyes of your most forbidden lover
And its claws, I tell you its claws are gloved in fire.

You are waiting to hear its name spoken,
You have asked me a thousand times to speak it,
You who have hidden it, cast it off, killed it,
Loved it to death and sung your songs over it.

The red bird you wait for falls with giant wings—
A velvet cape whose royal colour calls us kings
Is the form it takes as, uninvited, it descends,
It is the Power and the Glory forever, Amen.

The Eye

I implode
into the shrinking centre of your sight;
at some signal I cannot detect
my atoms invade me, rush inward
to a rendezvous beyond my knowing
and are sucked to nothing.
You are pulling me in like a dying star
to know me outside of time and space,
so rapid I go and disappear
into your face,
into the small beloved island of your Eye.

I am a creature of such energies
you could not count
and such fears you could not count
and here in my own dwelling-place
I give way to the Terror
just beyond the door;
it is no more than a signal
soft as a muffled drum
and Lord I come, I come.

At some command beyond my telling
I explode to life and shout—
Nothing dies, not star, not moon.
A universe, merely, is making room
to contain (I don't know how or why)
the small beloved island of your Eye.

You Held Out the Light

You held out the light to light my cigarette
But when I leaned down to the flame
It singed my eyebrows and my hair;
Now it is always the same—no matter where
We meet, you burn me.
I must always stop and rub my eyes
And beat the living fire from my hair.

Dark Stars

Like seas we contain life
and somehow ever are contained
by stony shores of pain
around us sharply drawn,
and also the awful circle of the sun
     (though all the hands of the world
     bear us up from perfect dark
     to light, we long for night
     and furious earth, and death
the one condition of our birth).

I shed the clear blood
of my eye, the red blood
of my time, and I shed
white blood like a prayer.
Am I a system of coloured waters
out of wounds in rock and flesh?
Am I fluid now and no more fire?
Look, I have told myself, I am the sea
sustained by the silver limits within me,
far beaches, far shores struck with light
and what I take from pain is mine
and what you take is yours
     (we are the wild heart of stars
     and life is the dark song descending
     unbidden and unending,
     and we are warned of dangers like
     the falling of the sky
     and know we will die
     a thousand times;
     though loverough hands bear us
from perfect dark to light, there is
no end, really, to the night).

And beyond the freest reaches of our sight
are sterner seas with birds and waves, dark
stars, which we cannot contain, which

are not ours; and then the shores of pain
are all too sharply drawn
and also the awful circle of the sun.

Two Voices

"All that you suffer in my name
Will only cast you furious through space;
You cannot displace me or explain
The holy terror which is my face.
I tell you you must grow tall as seas
Lest you drown in me.
Fear me and I fade, I go.
In what long nights did you deride me
And send me into dawn with a shaky laugh!
Use me like this and I'll break you in half."

"Love, move me, cast me furious through space;
Love, bend me to your time—
Test and revise me, I fear your face!
What is here, what is with me now
Is mine."

Poem

It is not lost, it is moving forward always,
Shrewd, and huge as thunder, equally dark.
Soft paws kiss its continents, it walks
Between lava avenues, it does not tire.

It is not lost, tell me how can you lose it?
Can you lose the shadow which stalks the sun?
It feeds on mountains, it feeds on seas,
It loves you most when you are most alone.

Do not deny it, do not blaspheme it,
Do not light matches on the dark of its shores.
It will breathe you out, it will recede from you.
What is here, what is with you now, is yours.

The Name of the Place

This is the world as we have made it,
As you and I together made it.
Do not speak to me of evil,
We know all the secret names of evil.
Do not speak to me of sorrow,
We invented all the shades of sorrow.
In my heart unspeakable deeds are sleeping
And why I have not yet performed them
Is due only to the shifts of season.
This is the world as you and I made it
And we must enter it, endure.
There are unbearable things to bear,
There is a place I dare not speak of
And we have all been there.

But none of us have been there alone
Although it's a small place, fit only for one,
Like the thin black rib of a panther
Or the small receding eye of a dying whale,
Anyway, you know it well.

We each have a message to give to the other,
The size of the place, the colour of the place,
How to get in and out of it,
How long it is safe to remain,
But first of all its name.

I know the name of the place so well
That it's just now slipped my tongue,
But it doesn't matter as long as you
Tell me I have not been there alone.
All things are plotting to make us whole,
All things conspire to make us one.

The Compass

"Now, Miss, the first thing you gotta understand
is that the earth moves around the sun.
I tell you this to help you get ahead in life.
And the next thing is you gotta watch
your grammar, Miss, your grammar,
'cause that's important to get ahead in life.
And don't be afraid to face a big Congomeration
of people,
me, I'm not afraid even though I just got out
of the Hospitality,
because I know where I stand, Miss,
and everything's gotta go and come back home
like the tides."

"Now you give me a ship and I'll take her
to Germany or Africa, you name it
because I know how the Gulf Stream divides
the world in two,
and I'm not scared to cross the great Atitude;
yes Miss—Atitude—
they say the Atlantic but I know
it's the Atitude,
'cause you go down the Longitude to reach
the Atitude, you follow me?"

"Stars? Sure, I can sail by the North Star
and the South Star
and the East Star
and the West Star.
Even on this train, Miss
you don't know it but we be sailing
by those stars
'cause they're the compass points
for all the world.
See this compass, you turn five degrees
and then you come back home.
You gotta always come back home, Miss,

like the tides."

"Look now, you be always at the centre,
even in a big Congomeration of people,
and all the words you talk here
go down to the sea, and the tide
brings 'em back tomorrow morning.
I tell you this so you won't fear
and you always know just where you stand
and how you're turning."

He turned the old German compass
over and over in his sure black hands.
"I had this fifteen years," he said,
"but I give it to you now so you
can get ahead in life,
and learn the Longitudes and Atitudes
and figure out just where you stand."

All I could think of
to give him in return
was my book of poems—a pointless gift.
But taking it he smiled and said,
"*I've* been doing some writing too
to get ahead in life!"
And pulled out from a suitcase old
as the crazy seas he sailed
something he handled with great respect—
a battered notebook where he'd written
in big scared lines
the first few letters of the alphabet.

FREDERICTON-HALIFAX, 1968

Reviresco: In Memory of Padraig O'Broin

Padraig, all of us were seeking
Lost languages, our own stolen tongues,
But I, young then, was speechless
When you read poems in Gaelic
And polished their metre
In the winters of Canada,
      and we sat, bards about
      a table, discussing craft;
      you careful, meticulous, gave
      green words of Ireland which I
      had never known
(I cast about, always, for another tongue).
      I never went to the land of my Scotch fathers,
      The snows of Canada long ago claimed me,
      I went east and south but never greenward,
      I went in and out but there was no road homeward.
I told you once that my family crest
Was a tree that grew from a rock—
Reviresco, We Will Flourish
Was the motto my ancestors bore,
      (but did I add that I had understood
      the split rock of my birth
      and nothing more?)
We wait so long to speak the truth.
Today I take the silver crest
And pin it on my coat,
      I don't know yet what it means to me,
      for I have only seen the rock split, Padraig,
Will you tell me later
the meaning of the tree?

The Heel

In the organing dark I bless those who came from the waters
scaleless and shrewd, and walked with unwebbed feet
to create memory, when every movement invented their end,
who stood beside the holy waters with upright spines
to destroy themselves, to inherit themselves, to stand
while the fish fell back and the waves erased their birth.

They were terrible with sense and torn at the tongue
and in the foreign hours when fog enveloped them
they thrashed like swimmers down the rivers of their sleep;
the sunken cities within them rose and towered high
over the bright groin of their pain, and elsewhere
they were lovers and their knees were pyramids of fire.

I bless those who turned the double face of memory around,
who turned on their naked green heels and had great dreams
and in the queer hour when they are struck at the eyes
and the last sunrise claims and cripples them, I stand
and remark that on the edge of this strand I also feel
the holy waters lapping just behind my heel.

The Discovery

do not imagine that the exploration
ends, that she has yielded all her mystery
or that the map you hold
cancels further discovery

I tell you her uncovering takes years,
takes centuries, and when you find her naked
look again,
admit there is something else you cannot name,
a veil, a coating just above the flesh
which you cannot remove by your mere wish

when you see the land naked, look again
(burn your maps, that is not what I mean),
I mean the moment when it seems most plain
is the moment when you must begin again

The Portage

We have travelled far with ourselves
and our names have lengthened;
    we have carried ourselves
on our backs, like canoes
in a strange portage, over trails,
insinuating leaves
and trees dethroned like kings,
    from water-route to
    water-route
seeking the edge, the end,
the coastlines of this land.

On earlier journeys we
were master ocean-goers
going out, and evening always found us
spooning the ocean from our boat,
    and gulls, undiplomatic
    couriers brought us
cryptic messages from shore
till finally we sealords vowed
we'd sail no more.

Now under a numb sky, sombre
cumuli weigh us down;
the trees are combed for winter
and bears' tongues have melted
all the honey;
    there is a lourd
suggestion of thunder;
subtle drums under
the candid hands of Indians
are trying to tell us
why we have come.

But now we fear movement
and now we dread stillness;
we suspect it was the land

that always moved, not our ships;
we are in sympathy with the fallen
trees; we cannot relate
        the causes of our grief.
We can no more carry
our boats our selves
over these insinuating trails.

Night on Gull Lake

One island
small as a wish invited us
and the lip of our borrowed boat
scraped it like a kiss;
          our first thought was:
how many travellers before us
had claimed it, given it
a name? Or could we be
the first? Why
          did it matter so much?

Feathers and feathers fell
or so it seemed, from high
invisible gulls; our unpiratable
ship was moored to a twig;
          there was nothing to steal
from it or the island. By night
the meagre tree held a star
in its fingers; we searched
for absences, and found at last
the sinuous absence
of a snake in the grass.

It was so simple, yet
it was not. What
          did we want?
We waited so long for morning
through the night of rain
which pinned us shivering against
a single rock,
and danced for joy before the dawn
when we made a miracle of fire from
some damp, protesting branches
that cracked as we stole them
          from the tree;
it was decided victory.

When we took off over
the shallow waves next day
        our pockets were full
of pebbles that we knew
we'd throw away,
and when we turned around
to see the island
one last time, it was lost
in fog and it
had never quite been found.

I Should Have Predicted

I should have predicted the death of this city;
I could have predicted it if only
there had been no such pretty flowers,
no such squares filled with horses
and their golden riders.

By this I mean that outside all was tame
and lucky, but inside, O inside houses
were wilder things—dynasties, wars,
empires crumbling, chariots housed
in halls, emperors in cupboards,
queens and generals in beds,
kingdoms rising and falling between the sheets.

Thus I did not predict the death of this city;
I was deceived by fountains and apple trees;
how could I know what civil wars raged inside
out of my sight, which focused only
on the horses and the gold, deceptive city?

Letter to a Future Generation

we did not anticipate you, you bright ones
though some of us saw you kneeling behind our bombs,
we did not fervently grow towards you
for most of us grew backwards
sowing our seed in the black fields of history

avoid monuments, engrave our names beneath your own
for you have consumed our ashes by now
for you have one quiet mighty language by now

do not excavate our cities
to catalogue the objects of our doom
but burn all you find to make yourselves room,
you have no need of archaeology,
your faces are your total history

for us it was necessary to invent a darkness,
to subtract light in order to see,
for us it was certain death to know our names
as they were written in the black books of history

I stand with an animal at my left hand
and a warm, breathing ghost at my right
saying, Remember that this letter was made
for you to burn, that its meaning lies
only in your burning it,
that its lines await your cleansing fire—
understand it only insofar
as that warm ghost at my right hand breathed
down my blood and for a moment wrote the lines
while guns sounded out from a mythical city
and destroyed the times

Inside the Great Pyramid

all day the narrow shaft
received us; everyone
came out sweating and
gasping for air, and one
old man collapsed
upon a stair;
        I thought:
the fact that it has stood
so long
is no guarantee
it will stand today,
but went in anyway
and heard when I was
halfway up a long
low rumbling like
the echo of ancient stones
first straining to their place;
        I thought:
we have made this, we
have made *this*.
I scrambled out into
the scandalous sun and saw
the desert was an hourglass
we had forgotten to invert,
a tasselled camel falling
to his knees, the River
filling the great waterclock
of earth.

Dark Pines Under Water

This land like a mirror turns you inward
And you become a forest in a furtive lake;
The dark pines of your mind reach downward,
You dream in the green of your time,
Your memory is a row of sinking pines.

Explorer, you tell yourself this is not what you came for
Although it is good here, and green;
You had meant to move with a kind of largeness,
You had planned a heavy grace, an anguished dream.

But the dark pines of your mind dip deeper
And you are sinking, sinking, sleeper
In an elementary world;
There is something down there and you want it told.

Song for a Stranger

Once every season for several years
You've entered the house of my sleep
And your coming alters the portents
Of the times. You know you have
A right to be there, and are admitted
Where others pause in fright, for you
Do not acknowledge any doors.

It's not only my dream but yours as well
(I know when you speak, I know when you call).
There are fields and halls, pavilions, hills,
Places with great pillars, pools.
We meet unplanned, each of us sure
The other will be there; it was written,
You see, long before.
We smile, we swim in turquoise pools
And then lie down together to plot
The birth of a more accurate world.

When I wake the first song of the city
Reveals your presences everywhere;
I am resolved in human time, and all
These seasons plot to draw you back
Into my dream. Stranger,
Do not let my sleep grow tame.

Dream Three: The Child

He was turning and turning and turning and turning
outside my window on a big unicycle
suspended in air beside a black tree.

Hey, why are you turning and turning and turning
getting nowhere fast on that wheel
when you could be talking to me?

I've always been here, turning and turning
and I'll always be here, turning and turning
From the beginning and to the end turning,
from alpha to omega turning and turning,
and I looked and I saw it was me.

We Are Sitting on a High Green Hill

and how we got here I cannot tell;
I have a basket and a little flute
which I play to coax the flowers out;
we call each other by quiet secret names
and our clothes are poor but our hair is tame
      —we are neither bad nor good
        and below us is a dark green wood.

we dream of the big world we cannot enter
and we sit till we silently turn into winter;
the fruit is all gone and our shoes are thin;
by night we lie down to let the darkness in
      —it is only by night that I cannot bear
        the cold, or the tired clothes we wear.

we dream of the big world we cannot enter
and we have no money and we turn into winter;
when the next spring comes we will melt until
we run like rivers down the high green hill.

The Last Day

Today is the last day of my life;
I knew it from the moment I awoke and saw
Sunlight on a small brass vase
And what is true is that which never was.

Now is the last hour of my life;
I rush back, midnight, I rush back to you—
I was a cascade of laughter, a trader in knives,
A London urchin, someone's lost shoe.

This is the last minute of my life;
It must be simple, it must be raw.
Sunlight strikes the small brass vase
And what is true is that which never was.

First Song from The Fifth Earth

*"By saying 'Love' you let loose all the angels
and demons that were asleep within the bowels
of mankind. 'Love' is not, as you think, a
simple, tranquil word. Within it lie armies
being massacred, burning cities and much blood.
Rivers of blood, rivers of tears: the face of the
earth has changed."*

Nikos Kazantzakis:
The Last Temptation of Christ

I say all worlds, all times, all loves are one
for we were there at the gathering of the waters
when our unborn hours gathered wave on wave
and our ages rose as seven sea-horses
far as our far-sight saw.
      (cruel rumours of time divide us
      world from world, and I am told
      it is the fifth earth where now
      we stand. But look, I want
      to walk in circles like the sun—
      don't ask why, take my hand!)
Of certain days and certain years
we will remember not a thing; time is
the ringing foam beneath the horses' hooves, and
our several lives are lost in their dark manes.
      (but it is out of this earth only
      that I begin to sing
      and another thing I cannot do
      and another song I cannot bring together,
      for I said we were there
      at the *gathering* of the waters)
All earths, all ages, and all loves are one,
but you say these maps are different,
this landscape has been changed,
      (angel, look again—
      it is only that these seas are blood,
      this continent the torso of

a tougher god than we can name)
Quickly, take my hand!
    (otherwise, it is all the same)

The Love-Clock

Love becomes the looking clock,
the listening clock of our days.
Becomes
the deep fugue of the sun, and
the length of our shadows.
Becomes the shadow
of two trees against sand
and the listening of the trees
and the looking of the sand.

And love becomes the whole
listening earth and the length
of all shadows,
and what we have gained
from this listening
and this ticking
is a knowledge of time,
that only.

Love becomes the looking clock,
the beautiful catastrophes of morning,
the listening of two trees standing.

The Kingdom

The lame the blind the marred the broken
saith the master will enter
my unspeakable kingdom,
and I have spoken knowing not
what is the kingdom.

I have killed with the flagrant tools
of death, and the very word
of death sounds itself behind love
and I have harkened to it knowing not
what is the kingdom.

the lame the blind the marred the broken
saith the master will enter
my unspeakable heart
to die there first before the kingdom
to hurt, to part.

I have broken love open
to clip and freeze the arteries of its blood.
I am the lame the blind the marred the broken
minister of pain
and keeper of the final kingdom;
talk me into it, word of death, again.

The Sacrifice

I considered too long
the leaves and their golden
falling (these
sacrifices, these
necessary deaths),
until at last I came to see
how my people were dropping
one by one
their golden moments
to the ground,
and offering up the holy
oil of all their loves
to burn black and sour
at what insufferable
altars of the world,
the dizzy smoke encircling
their yearning hands,
their loins,
and the voices of my people
turning into feeble echoes
as they let their truest
prayers
drop sadly to the ground
and called instead
for some shapeless
ghost
to consecrate and take
these gifts,
these living
offerings
they didn't need to make.

Now I can't watch a man rake
leaves in autumn, for I think
of that other,
unnecessary season
when the Gardener comes to gather

all the living leaves
     (these best
     of our dreams)
we let fall
one by one
deliberately.

Did we think
that by killing
our golden
selves, O
God,
we were somehow
gathering Thee?

The Shadow-Maker

I have come to possess your darkness, only this.

My legs surround your black, wrestle it
As the flames of day wrestle night
And everywhere you paint the necessary shadows
On my flesh and darken the fibres of my nerve;
Without these shadows I would be
In air one wave of ruinous light
And night with many mouths would close
Around my infinite and sterile curve.

Shadow-maker create me everywhere
Dark spaces (your face is my chosen abyss),
For I said I have come to possess your darkness,
Only this.

The Armies of the Moon

now they begin to gather their forces
in the Marsh of Decay and the Sea of Crises;
their leaders stand motionless
on the rims of the craters
invisible and silver as swords turned sideways
waiting for earthrise and the coming of man.

they have always been there increasing their numbers
at the foot of dim rills, all around and under
the ghostly edges where moonmaps surrender
and hold out white flags to the night.

when the earthmen came hunting with wagons and golfballs
they were so eager for white rocks and sand
that they did not see them, invisible and silver
as swords turned sideways on the edge of the craters—
so the leaders assumed they were blind.

in the Lake of Death there will be a showdown;
men will be powder, they will go down under
the swords of the unseen silver armies,
become one with the gorgeous anonymous moon.

none of us will know what caused the crisis
as the lunar soldiers reluctantly disband
and return to their homes in the Lake of Dreams
weeping quicksilver tears for the blindness of man.

The Hunt

my cat goes *behind* the shadows
into the majestic dark of shoes
or cryptic corners where the spirits hide;
for me too this house is not
a mere conspiracy of walls, but
a jungle of eyes, the lost worlds
of the Kalahari, King Solomon's mines.

I know exactly what he's hunting down
day after day in the dark places—
dream creatures with fluorescent eyes
which shine like jewels
in the caves of his awakening.

on the television screen
two ghostly blobs of men dissolve
on the rim of a lunar crater,
and I know exactly what they're hunting down
hour after hour in the seas without water.

now the astronauts are journeying
over the rim of my sleep
and this red-eyed cat dissolves in air;
if you are looking for me now, my Hunter,
you will not find me here.

Meditations of a Seamstress (1)

When it's all too much to handle
and the green seams of the world start fraying,
I drink white wine and sew
like it was going out of style;
      curtains become dresses, dresses
become pillowcovers, clothes
I've worn forever get taken in or out.
Now I can't explain exactly
what comes over me, but when the phone rings
I tell people I'm indisposed;
I refuse to answer the door, I even
neglect my mail.
      (Something vital is at stake,
the Lost Stitch or the Ultimate Armhole,
I don't know what) and hour after hour
on the venerable Singer
I make strong strong seams for my dresses
and my world.
      The wine possesses me
and I sew like a fiend, forgetting to use
the right colours of thread, unable to make
a single straight line;
I know somehow I'm fighting time
and if it's not all done by nightfall
everything will come apart again;
continental shelves will slowly drift into the sea
and earthquakes will tear wide open
the worn-out patches of Asia.

Dusk, a dark needle, stabs the city
and I get visions of chasing fiery spools of thread
mile after mile over highways and fields
until I inhabit some place at the hem of the world
where all the long blue draperies
of skies and rivers wind;
      spiders' webs describe
the circling of their frail thoughts forever;

everything fits at last and someone has lined
the thin fabric of this life I wear with grass.

Meditations of a Seamstress (2)

I dream impossible clothes which will confess me
and fall apart miraculous as the Red Sea
to reveal to you the stunning contours of my
mind (you who wear the world with a grace
I will never achieve, invisibly,
like the arcane garment of the emperor).
I dream things not to be worn in this city,
yards of silks which like Isadora's scarf
may one day choke me, blue tunics held together
by buckles bearing the portraits of lost kings,
vests carved from the skin of frightened deer,
green velvet cloaks in which I may soundlessly collapse
and succumb to the Forest, sleeves to stress
the arm of the archer, the huntress, Artemis.

Only one dress I made ever came out right—
(it will never happen that way again);
all the way down the front of it
where it opens from the collar to the hem
I sewed the signs of Athens,
a row of obsolete but perfect keys
on a strip of black and gold,
with which you may, O naked emperor,
enter and decode my world.

Sea Things

I've been giving a lot of thought
to shellfish and sponges and those
half-plant half-animal things that go
flump flump on the seafloor, also
a funny thing shaped like a pyramid
which spends all its life
buried in the sand upside-down
and has no friends.

And because I know nothing
about the sea I worry
about how they're finding their food
or making love, or for that matter
if they have anything to make love with.

I open a can of oysters
and see them all lying there, lying there
naked and embryonic, and wonder
how long I can go on worrying about things
that creep around miles below my eye
beneath tons of black water

With their hopes and fears and hungers
and their attempts to better themselves
and the secret brains or pearls they keep
protected in their shells.

I've been giving them a lot of thought
but I do not really want to know them,
for they flung me forth, a nuisance in their midst
with my mind and complex hungers
crashing on the high white beaches of the world.

Dining at the Savarin

because I too have come to partake of this awesome buffet
determined to get my money's worth by going back again
and again to refill my plate even when
I no longer hunger

I cannot wonder
why the man at the next table eats so much, what
secret doubt he soothes with the impossible pyramid
of food before his eyes

because I cannot presume
to know his pain, yet know it so well it is my own
I eat in shame

yet I'm amazed
with what venom I crack open the corpse of this white crab
the sound like a bark of protest from some pre-human world
and how loudly I suck the sweet meat from the hollow
of its claw

casting furtive glances
at the others who dine in this enormous room, choking
down such terrible love and pity as I cannot presume
to recapture here

and because I cannot know
their hunger, yet know it so well it is my own
I revisit the bright buffet in a kind of dream
and pile my tired plate

with primeval things—
smoked oysters, scarlet lobsters, shining shrimps,
telling myself that seafood is very good for the brain
and creep back again

to the table, that wreck of my former hunger, to devour
the guts and claws of creatures which preceded me

and still survive

as the organist plays those old songs we know so well
we have forgotten, and I pray to the god of men and lobsters
and all things that die and do not die

forgive me this second
unreal hunger, Lord of the infinite buffet

Memoirs of a Mad Cook

There's no point kidding myself any longer,
I just can't get the knack of it; I suspect
there's a secret society which meets
in dark cafeterias to pass on the art
from one member to another.
Besides,
it's so *personal* preparing food for someone's
insides, what can I possibly *know*
about someone's insides, how can I presume
to invade your blood?
I'll try, God knows I'll try
but if anyone watches me I'll *scream*
because maybe I'm handling a tomato wrong,
how can I *know* if I'm handling a tomato wrong?

something is eating away at me
with splendid teeth

Wistfully I stand in my difficult kitchen
and imagine the fantastic salads and soufflés
that will never be.
Everyone seems to grow thin with me
and their eyes grow black as hunters' eyes
and search my face for sustenance.
All my friends are dying of hunger,
there is some basic dish I cannot offer,
and you my love are almost as lean
as the splendid wolf I must keep always
at my door.

Lilith

Have no doubt that oneday she will be reborn
horrendous, with coiling horns,
pubis a blaze of black stars
and armpits a swampy nest for dinosaurs.
But meanwhile
she lurks in her most impenetrable disguise—
as me—
trying to make holes in my brain
or come forth from my eyes.
And I have felt
her mindless mind within my mind
urging me to call down heaven with a word,
avenge some ancient wrong against her kind
or be the crazed Salome who danced for blood.
Ah God, her seasons kill
the sickly moon, and all my fine achievements
fall beneath her feet like skulls.
And I would claim
I cannot answer for my deeds—it is *her time*.
But when I try
to prove she is assailing me
there comes instead an awful cry
which is her protest and her song of victory.
See you in my *dreams,*
Whore of Babylon, Theodora,
utterly unquiet fiend, thou
Scream.

The Vacuum Cleaner Dream

I dreamt I was vacuuming the universe
and everything got sucked
into my blind machine
     whirr whirr whirr
I was an avenging angel
and the best cleaning woman
in the world.

I dreamt I was vacuuming
with a sickening efficiency
and everything went into
the head of the extra-galactic vacuum beast,
expertly tamed by me,
avenging angel
and the best cleaning woman
in the world.

And when I opened the bag
to empty it I found:
a dictionary of dead tongues
a bottle of wine
lunar dust
the rings of Saturn
and the sleeping body of my love.

Flight One

Good afternoon ladies and gentlemen
This is your Captain speaking.

We are flying at an unknown altitude
And an incalculable speed.
The temperature outside is beyond words.

If you look out your windows you will see
Many ruined cities and enduring seas
But if you wish to sleep please close the blinds.

My navigator has been ill for many years
And we are on Automatic Pilot; regrettably
I cannot foresee our ultimate destination.

Have a pleasant trip.
You may smoke, you may drink, you may dance
You may die.
We may even land oneday.

Phobos

Last week lightning clove the mighty tree
outside my house, and the leaves turned in
surrendering their white sides; I learned
that lightning cleaves what it most loves
and cuts in half what it means to caress

Nothing is safe nothing is safe anymore
and the stronger I become the more I fear
I will invite the deadly kiss of wind
or water, air or fire, which will slay me
lay me out like the corpse under yellow plastic
I saw once off the highway in a ditch

Nothing is safe nothing is safe anymore
and I am sure the silver jet which crashed
last week at dawn leaving *parts* of bodies
on the ground, was a thing the earth found lovely
and called down, merely *called down* to embrace

I'm terrified of cars and planes and weather
and fear itself which only makes me stronger
as I walk like a broken child through scared streets
through the wicked rubble of unspeakable nights

It will come to us when we are strong
because it *loves us* it will mow us down

I turn in now, surrendering my white side
to the horror which will one day claim me

Nor would I be at all surprised
to wake up tomorrow and espy
the loaf of bread upon my table
sliced by the swords of the samurai

Note from a Figure at Pompeii

the world ends here, but
it has ended every moment of my life;
I tell you not to fear
agony. is this cataclysm only
the jealous kiss of God?

this question I put to the impervious stones.

there have been warnings
but no one has heeded them;
here as I feel the seasons bend
I do violence to myself. perhaps
I want to be ready on my knees
when the fire comes.

if I continue to visualize this end
I will surely bring it about;
I will believe in mind over matter
as matter consumes me.

you will know me when you find me;
I am the figure to the left of the boulder
half-raised on my hands, a petrified
awakening, my self turned stone

as I achieve this bitter victory
too late, as all victories are—
this conquest of my reluctant self,
this final freedom from my fear.

The Child Dancing

there's no way I'm going to write about
the child dancing in the Warsaw ghetto
in his body of rags

there were only two corpses
on the pavement that day
and the child I will not write about
had a face as pale and trusting
as the moon

(so did
the boy with a green belly full of dirt
lying by the roadside
in a novel of Kazantzakis
and the small girl T. E. Lawrence wrote about
who they found after the Turkish massacre
with one shoulder chopped off, crying:
"don't *hurt* me, Baba!")

I don't feel like slandering them with poetry.

the child who danced
in the Warsaw ghetto
to some music no one else could hear
had moon-eyes, no
green horror and no fear
but something worse

a simple desire to please
the people who stayed
to watch him shuffle back and forth,
his feet wrapped in the newspapers
of another ordinary day

The Other Underground

who will absolve me of the crimes
which I commit each night in dreams?
not you, my dark associates
who shade your eyes with many flags
and do not see these nests of lightning
in the trees.

I am so far underground you cannot find me;
I fight with strange and silver armies, all
ideologies enrage me;
I have no plots against the system,
having taken many years
to overthrow myself.

you have not noticed that all wars
are happening inside my head,
you have not asked me to get out of Vietnam,
the conflagration which is the Asia of my mind
where I commit, alone,
the atrocities of my time

tell me what the dark committees of my soul are plotting
and where the guerillas of my guilt are hiding out—
for I remember that the cockpit of the plane
was silent in Hiroshima,
as silent as my skull, O silent
was my skull before eyes bled from heads,
dripped out or melted inward,
before the man sitting in the sun somewhere
dissolved and left the black atomic shadow
of his soul upon the stairs.

it's too late to argue about who
has seen the light; nobody has a monopoly
on light. I cannot dazzle you with data or compare
tyrants and liberators who eventually become
tyrants.

I cannot discuss politics,
only your dreams and my bloody hands.

the midnights lit by warlight, scarlet stars,
the sheer hallucination of our wars
have somehow grown from small hurts, symbolic
murders,
and the tyranny is with us everyday
in our small cruel lies,
in our turning away from love,
and the Enemy is where he always was—
in the bleak lunar landscapes of our mirrors.

I'm so far underground you cannot find me,
hating the untellable which must get told,
trying to read the monthly Morse-code of the moon,
these urgent letters to the world.

It Comes Upon You

It comes upon you suddenly that this is its moment,
This is what it's all been for, the secret
That you held in store like a juggler always allowing for
The ball that is not there.

It comes upon you suddenly that to sit here
With cold coffee and the day's penultimate cigarette
Is the sum total of all the painful becoming
And the Hell. If you can't see it now you never will.

It comes upon you suddenly that you must wear
The many selves you gathered and regrew
With a kind of pride and poise that falsifies their weight
With cool deceptive ease

Or else cry forever as once before you cried
On a high hill overlooking everything; God
Withdraw my fingers from your hair and break my eyes!

103

The Film

I think I must have been with you
in all the movie-houses of the world,
or else you perform
in the dark theatres of my blood
parts you never meant to play;
        did you watch too long
those Universal spectacles
of wars where nobody ever dies,
of monstrous lovers who kiss forever
        down the corridors
of Time?
The fervent curtains fall apart
and the silver screen is skin.

I think the walls of the place you live in
whisper names and legends in the night,
and wispy film unwinds, unwinds
in some unseen projector run
by a cruel Technician who merely wants
        to drive you blind
and send his Cast of Thousands
clanging through your sleep.

I think that when you raise your hand
against those walls
your flesh becomes a screen,
        the drama unfolds
along your fingers
and across your open palm the armies run
and down your veins their false blood falls;
        I want to tell you—
Look this is the kind of war nobody needs.
But now the images have claimed your face,
        you are alive with lies and legends,
the silver reel unravels in your skull,
the dark film roars forever down your blood.

The Telescope Turned Inward

the telescope turned inward
to the corner of the room
is slowly falling into inner space
alone,
the lens like your dead eye
which fell away from stars
turns in to the vivid zero
of your dreams,
the place where nightmares
burst like bladders
or nova suns.
Goodbye, goodbye,
the planets have resigned
and left me all alone;
you have collapsed to a microcosm
where your brilliant secrets
no more masquerade as stars,
there are no more galaxies
there is no more moon;
above me the vast necropolis of space,
below, a telescope turned inward
and silver dust I must sweep up tomorrow
in the corner of the room.

Jewellery

I wear it more to be its captive
than to captivate; I want
to be the prisoner of gold,
to hear my voice break through
the chain which holds my song
in check, or watch the tendons
flicker under
the band about my wrist
which makes my gestures
conscious and restrained;
the circular earrings
familiar as my name
have tamed my mind
as the single ring
has tamed my hand.

You have made a glittering prison
of all my jewellery,
you knew I never wanted
to be free.

The Sign

What you have finally made me do
is trace with my foot
in the frightened dirt
the sacred fish, the Christian
calling-card, the sign
of the society, that all may know
I am one to go down
to the secret feasts
beneath the aqueducts of Rome.

You think that this is my surrender to
some quieter form of love
and that this thin and spineless fish
swims only in rock or dust.

But what I am learning
is the lust of God,
the seas which boil in the bones,
and when next time I get to you
the teeth of my kiss
will trace in your flesh
the holy symbol of the catacombs.

Hypnos

He lies there in a wilderness of sheets
and his body inhabits strange spaces, oblique
dimensions;
      like the keen emptiness of a child's eye
      it offers me no entry and no alibi.
Horses (I think) charge into
the white night of his sleep.
He celebrates the birthdays of his dreams
and does not know I ponder
how I might join him there.

Yet I fear to even if I could
for in his sleep he is powerful
as a withheld word.

He lies there accomplished and unknown,
his limbs arranged by passion and by art,
a fluid beauty he inhabits all alone.
The dark bird of war is dormant in his loins
and prophets reside in the seeds of his kiss;
      the generations of his mouth are legion
      yet his body is inviolably his.

He may lie, he may live there forever
and I can say nothing of the meaning of this sleeper.

Credo

I believe it all because
no one can tell me that
the Dancer in my blood is
dead; also, my fingerprints are
the landscapes of ten unknown moons.
Also I ask you what could be stupider
than a world without a world.
Believing everything, I do not expect
you to believe an untenable myth
or this incredible lie
which is slowly turning you into truth.

The Hour of the Singer

Your life falls away from the mouth of the singer
and you are left with one song you must sing forever;
all you have aspired to you have already done
or seen in the eyes of the indestructible One.
     This is the hour when it all falls away
and you are lost in the blind mouth of the singer
and everything you ever wanted is contained
in the naked pause between his words.
     Through his red music he smiles to warn you
you have always moved among the gods.

All you have sought you have already found
and now it falls away beyond the sounding hours
of the blood and the years of false singing.
     What you have been is a tale beyond telling
and all that has fallen away from his mouth and your life
is yours forever, without ending.

Now you comprehend your first and final lover
in the dark receding planets of his eyes,
and this is the hour when you know moreover
that the god you have loved always
will descend and lie with you in paradise.

Arcanum One: The Prince

and in the morning the king loved you most
and wrote your name with a sun and a beetle
and a crooked ankh, and in the morning
you wore gold mainly, and the king adorned you
with many more names.

beside fountains, both of you slender
as women, circled and walked together
like sunrays circling water, both of you
slender as women wrote your names with
beetles and with suns, and spoke together
in the golden mornings.

and the king entered your body
into the bracelet of his name
and you became a living syllable
in his golden script, and your body
escaped from me like founting water
all the daylong.

but in the evenings you wrote my name
with a beetle and a moon, and lay upon me
like a long broken necklace which had fallen
from my throat, and the king loved you
most in the morning, and his glamorous love
lay lengthwise along us all the evening.

Arcanum Two: The Conspirator

my brother, you board the narrow boat and the river owns
    you
over and over; why do you sail like this between your sister
and the distant king? my chamber is full of politics
and hunger. why do you go to him? his chin is thin
and his thighs bulge. why do you go to the king your father?

your boat, your narrow boat goes forth each morning
and snouts of crocodiles worry the water.
why do you go each morning after
our bodies make narrow rivers together?

I know how you plot against the king your father
whose thighs flung you forth as from a salty river;
you will steal the crown which bulges from his head
and mount the thin throne which no one holds forever.

O do not go to the king our father
but stay in this house beside the worried river;
there are a thousand kingdoms yet to conquer
in the narrow nights when we lie together,
and the distant king on his thin and hungry throne
can neither live nor lie nor sing forever.

Arcanum Three: The Death of the Prince

He was employed upon the marble floor
Between the fountain and the pillars.
        They looked for him, the silvery guards
        Sought him all daylong, and my brother
Did not hear them calling through the halls.

And finding him employed upon the marble floor
They fell before him crying: Majesty!
        (Lord, his mouth was terrible
        And his cheek a granite cliff)
And he lifted up his head and smiled.

He was destroyed upon the marble floor
Between the fountain and the pillars
        And I bent over him to call his name,
        His secret name whose syllables were thunder—
Then I took the heavy crown and threw it in the river.

Arcanum Four: The Embalming

along your body strips of gold unroll
your name which caused a kingdom's fall
and your wrapped ribs, my silent one,
refuse the sun, and down your legs run
legends of the night. in white cloth I wound you
in your final house beside the water
and I know the gates are locked forever,
the gates of light are locked forever
as my loins lock, as the river.

in white cloth bound, and blind
you breathe in death the winds of night
as the sweet stiff corpse of your petrified
sex points upward into heaven
in your tomb beside the river,
though the gates of light are locked forever,
the legs and lips of light are locked forever.

my fingers twice have traced
your name all down your flesh, and they
have dipped its signs in water.
now sleep my blind, my silent brother
as my womb locks, as the river,
your tomb a virgin by jackals sealed
and the gates of light are locked forever.

Arcanum Five: The Prayer

death is a snake on your smashed brow
but still I beg you to get up and go
beyond the drowning river where your crown lies
towards the sighing house of reeds where I
stand waiting in the hollow doorway of eternity.

O brother, from your tomb arise! your bones
are targets in a hunter's eyes, your soul
the naked arrow which he fires.

in the name of our father, by the ring he wore,
come touch this floor with feet that burned
a thousand times the grass between the river
and this fervent house.
as bird arise, as arrow! and tomorrow
let the strips of linen fall.
all your limbs are tombs of sorrow.
I beg you now, my silent brother
to crash those gates which are not locked forever.
O bless and break them ten times over!

Arcanum Six: The Centuries

I waited two millennia in the house beside the river
calling to the north wind many times over,
and feeding doves, and laying fruit beside your tomb
which thieves and beggars stole by night in summer,
and burning prayers and perfume on the hungry altar.
elsewhere slept our mad forgotten father
and the land fell into wretchedness, and later
watersnakes and foreign boats profaned the river.

and sometimes you visited as bird the thirsty bed
where we had lain, and hovered above and said,
"I will come back in better forms than this,
my sister, but the gates are hard to break,
so hard to break you cannot know
and death is like the long sleep after love
when nothing can persuade the limbs to move."

your tired wings were songs among the leaves
and on my thighs you left your shining, unreal seed.

and other centuries I do not try to count
with doves and thieves and moons appeared and went,
with stars that wrote strange warnings in the skies.
the eyes of many kingdoms closed, the palace was defiled
by princes with strange-coloured eyes.

brother, I awaited the end of all the world.

Arcanum Seven: The Return

now as I wear around my neck a necklace
of a million suns, you come
undead, unborn, thou Ghost of the morning!

I notice that you wear our father's ring
but I must say no more
for the bed of ebony and straw
lies like a fallen song upon the floor
where last we left it, broken with love and bare.
the world will loathe our love of salt and fire
and none will let you call me sister here.

see how my body bears the mouthmarks made
in times long past, star-wounds in night unhealed;
since then it was a cave by jackals sealed.
but now my legs are once more cages
for a great far-flying bird, my breasts
small pyramids of love, my mouth
is empty of the dark wine of my waiting.

O tell me all the things you saw,
and call me sister
and bless this bed of ebony and straw.

Arcanum Eight: The Story

"sister, from the gates and fields of night I came
lured by your voice as it spoke my name
over water and fire, and the voice of him
who told me that his sun would burn forever.

"I'll tell you why I went each morning to the river
and sailed towards that old man on the throne.
his seed struggled in my reluctant thighs
and the ring on his hand was stone
and his eyes were the mirrors of the world
and he was the very lord of gold.

"so I went each morning to the king my father.
but all is told, I cannot tell another thing
about how his blood was the birth of my soul
and how with my own hands I killed the king, the king.

"now when the sun is born each day at dawn
I will lie along your body as a boat along a river
and place my soul a blazing ornament upon your breasts
and burn with my bones my name all down your flesh.
sister, by a dark love bound and blind
I touch you now, in this forbidden time
and my white robes of death unwind."

Arcanum Nine: The Ring

I do not adorn you with any more names
for the living ghost of the king our father
hovers forever above our secret bed
like the royal hawk with wings outspread
on whose head the awful sun burns out
the many generations of our dreams.

and we are the end of his ancient line,
your seed a river of arrested time
whose currents bring the cursed crown
forever back to the foot of this bed—
the double crown of those who wear
the kingdoms of heaven and hell on their head.

the royal bird is blind in morning
and its glamorous wings will shade us
till the end of time. but O my brother
will you wear forever that stolen ring
which wounds your hand by night, and why
in your dreams do you go to the king, the king?

Part Two: Magic Animals, 1972-1974

1

Watch me
I am moving through the cages of the animals
I am moving through the peereek of their cells
Watch me because
I am watching them watching you
They are holding your immortal souls in trust
They have watched you since Eden
They are waiting for their time

2

When the day bends over backwards
to bring forth the light
I must know by whose permission I inhabit this place
in the holy congregation of animals
and mortal stones

Nothing lives here that does not flaunt
the handsome secret of its death
Nothing dies here that does not first
defile the earth

This tree is sexier than anyone remembers
and the world was made
for flutes and Jews
for jackals and for bells

The sun though
Look
Denies our citadels

3
Not to worry

The birds falling from these nests into the mouths of
gorgeous cats are always falling from these nests like
lost particles of speech or the pared fingernails of
the Almighty

Make sure you know with certainty what day it is, and
why, to answer for all the green and falling things of
Earth

Neither break the afternoon into unequal parts nor heed
the false and orange gods who insinuate life

For we are green and ever falling from high nests of
wind, the secret houses of the sky, into the jaws of
gorgeous cats and flowers

Not to worry but be handsome and heed these

4

Lord, the night we danced on broken glass!
It was a time of oracles
and the blue world was slowly sinking into sand

I hid myself in the dangerous fur
of the Siamese cat who owned my house

I hid myself in the marvellous ear
of the fox who slept in my bureau drawer

Who in their sole mind would fear
the animals and the beastly gods
It is human nature I abhor

I said as we danced on broken glass
I said as I lapped up the cream of heaven
I said as the god became a cat
I said as the cat became a man

It was a time of oracles
and the blue world was slowly sinking into sand

5

Man the world is red as rust, crass, heavy, and thrice-blessed

The scrapings of the mad cicadas sing me into heaven

Come, you black trisexual god of beasts
ghost of the meridians
centaur who usurps my sleep

Play me the infamous music of the animals
Ring me the blood's bells, scarlet molecules

I need to be anointed by a foreign god
and disappear in a cloud of lies

I need to know the moose and beetles
will one day lose me and reclaim the earth

I need to hear an anthem played with hooves and horns

6

I led the beloved up limegreen stairs of air
to the garden of the sky horses   where

White beasts flanked the silly clouds
with great limegreen eyes   and their

pretty hooves wounded heaven

God, I said, Ghost of air and Ghost of green—
for the first and last time I tell you
this is no dream I dream

7

My man digs into the eye of the lamb
with a fork and knife I carved from bone

I too have eaten lamb's head on several
occasions   the succulent mouth I suck

French kiss of my hunger   tongue whirling
round its juicy gums and tiny bestial teeth

French kiss of my hunger?   you cannot kiss
a living lamb   much less pluck out its creamy brain

with a fork and a knife you carved from bone

I resent these probings inside my head
and tell whoever's writing it to end
this tiny bestial poem

8

Everything I have seen here
I have failed to understand

Save perhaps the clean breath of cats,
perfume of leopard and lynx

A black goat taking notes on nothing
from behind an olive tree

It is too late to know anything
We have slammed and hammered
all the beautiful animals into heaven

Clueless I sing
the anthems of the beasts and sovereign stones

9

The orang-utang is having a fit
He flings his raisin bread sky high
He bashes his fists against the walls

The gorilla picks up his rubber tire
and holds it like an old black halo on his head

The baboons meanwhile are shaking the bars
The baboons are baring their awful teeth

But the mandrill with his mardi-gras mask
folds his arms and examines a world
more surreal than his rose-red ass

10

And when I look into the sane and skyblue minds of animals
I know where they hurt and what they love

From his cage the spider monkey
screams me his wretched secrets

They throw him blue balloons and lighted matches
They throw him melba toast and lies

And he looks me straight in the eye, the eye
with his phallus floating like a strange thin toadstool
in the air

Then hangs upside-down by his tail from heaven
dismissing my existence as a beastly lie

11

Dinner was a plate of broken birds
I could not eat   there is no heaven for the man or raven
perching on the bust of Poe

*

Yet I have feasted on succulent knuckles
braised by sun or bruised by fate,
feasted on these and lived

*

What is the love that kills and the love that contains?
One hot afternoon somewhere in the Aegean
a hunter came down from the hills with a string
of twitching yellow-red blue-green wings
and met his wife with her caged canary
which still had the gall to sing

*

Children are more violent than all
the pretty beasts and flowers

A small girl dug a grave for the dead pigeon
in the grass

And later disentombed the thing
and hacked the corpse to pieces
with the spade that she had hidden
till the last

12
Toronto Star, June 14, 1972

Police are looking for the killers of three flamingoes
apparently stoned to death Monday night at Storybrooke
Gardens in Springbank Park . . . the bodies of the
birds were found floating in their pond yesterday
morning.

I can snap their knees with tweezers
for their legs are very thin

I can burn their beaks with matches
to erase their silly grin

I can stone them in the darkness
for there's nothing else to do

I can accomplish all the icky things
I'd like to do to you

In a pinky pond 3 red flamingoes lie
slowly rotting on the beaches of my sanity

13

Here where the stars pretend
they do not know us

I bring an army of blotting paper
and of doves

Here where I fall to the ground like a stone
and all the wandering trees return

I sing the single everchanging Lord, who

threatens me with paradise

14

Who is this fool who threatens me with
paradise?

Everything resounds with birds, plums, whatever

The wounded vulture which resides
in these and other loins, endures

Without you carriers of black paradise—
carrion-crows, scare-birds, worms

Heed me as I heed you, scavengers
I have loved who scared me into hell
with paradise

I put to you a question you cannot refuse

What vulture's making time within
the mighty prison of your groins?

What dove gone mad, what
alien and everchanging Lord
sings me the anthems of the beasts and sovereign stones?

Genesis

In the Beginning God was mad, and He knew it.
He took no precautions and let His mighty sperm
spill out into gorgeous space.

Stars, stars all over the place!
And all His creations were acts of madness, and
He knew it and He felt afraid.

(Monstrous moonface of the ape He made,
unholy proof of my wildest dreams.)

Some men were animals who woke up and went sane.
Moonheads. And he decided to take vengeance
on them thus:

He bestowed upon them the Black Kiss which is
the jealous kiss of God.
This He bestowed upon the loud and hungry,
on those who knew He was mad and weren't ready
to let Him get away with it. Man, He was angry
because they wouldn't let Him get away with it!

Godfather.

Magic Cats *(With acknowledgements to Susan Musgrave, whose "Strawberry" poems started it all)*

* Most cats, with the exception of Burmese, do not celebrate their birthdays. Rather, they are extremely sentimental about Palm Sunday and Labour Day, at which times they survive solely on white lace and baloney sandwiches.

* Cats on the whole are loath to discuss God.

* Generally speaking, cats have no money, although some of them secretly collect rare and valuable coins.

* Cats believe that all human beings, animals and plants should congregate in a huge heap in the centre of the universe and promptly fall asleep together.

* Of all the cats I have known, the ones I remember most are: Bumble Bee, Buttonhole, Chocolate Bar, Molten Lava and Mushroom. I also remember Tabby who was sane as a star and spent all his time lying on his back in the sink, thinking up appropriate names for me.

* Cats see their Keepers as massive phantoms, givers of names and the excellent gravy of their days.

* Cats who have been robbed of balls and claws do not lament. They become their Keepers' keepers.

* When cats are hosts to fleas they assume the fleas are guests.

* Most cats would rather be covered with live fleas than dead ones.

* Cats hold no grudges and have no future. They invade nests of strangers with their eyes.

* The patron saint of cats is called: Beast of the Skies, Warm Presence, Eyes.

* Cats do not worry about the gurgling horrors of the diseases listed in catbooks, some of which are Hairballs Enteritis and Bronchitis. But they do become very upset about Symptoms, which is the worst disease of all.

* When cats grow listless (i.e. lose their list) they cease to entertain fleas. They mumble darkly about radishes and death. They listen to Beethoven and become overly involved in Medieval History.

* When cats decide to die   they lie alone   lost among leaves beneath the dark winds and broad thunders of the world and pray to the Beast of the Skies, Warm Presence, Eyes.

* Broadly speaking, cats do not read Gothic novels, although they tend to browse through Mary Shelley on the day before Christmas.

* The only reason cats do not carry passports is because they have no pockets.

* When a black cat crosses your path it usually means that he is trying to get to the other side of the street.

* Cats never get baptized. They lose their dry.

* Cats only perspire during Lent.

* Cats have no memory and no future. They are highly allergic to Prime Ministers, radishes, monks, poets, and death.

Plants I Have Known

What am I saying: I have never known a plant.
Yet I have many. They grow out of the walls, out
Of my ears.

They refuse to tell me their names, although
I often coax them with Bufferin and wine.

I have a Venus Fly-Trap who doesn't
And an orange cactus who won't
Tell me their names, although I cry
And threaten them with tea and poetry.

They thrive, they thrive. I hate them.
My cats chew idly on their thighs.
They couldn't care less about God
And sometimes neither can I.

And there's one green guy who lies
Vertically in the corner without eyes.
You know the plant I mean. You touch
His leaves and he promptly dies.

The Four Horses

I disappeared for years beneath these silly skies
Under the pretty ribs of birds
And trees who pretend they do not know me.

Night rides in on those skinny horses
And revelation never comes.

(There is a foreign ownership in the blood,
Just one of the wicked plans of God.)

With the purring of the doves, and me
Caught on the broad horns of morning,
The children are all ridden by bicycles
And the television watches me.

Nakedness is less naked than we presume.

I tell all the trees to go home.

Sea Images

The only thing to fear in the sea is yourself
said Ley the diver
In that case, come with us and find Atlantis
said I, half-joking
My dear, don't you know how deep you have to go
to find a single thing?
laughed Ley.

     *

Perhaps we are only dim figures underwater
meeting for a moment
the perfect eyes of fishes
which encounter us sideways
in luminous surprise

And perhaps on land we hang on
to our illnesses which protect us
from the full responsibility of health

And perhaps on land we do not have
to answer for our crimes
while undersea we answer
and the sea will answer for itself

     *

We speared the big red starfish because it was there
and when we brought it to the beach we saw
that one of its legs was dangling by a thread
neither on nor off.
We lay flat upon the sand watching it at eye-level
and wondering what we had wanted it for
—hostage of water—
and as we lay he slowly and deliberately broke away
leaving his big red leg behind him.
And as we lay and wondered he shuffled and limped

back into the sea
assuming full responsibility.

    *

What a lovely shell! I cried
and raced out of the water and placed in on a rock
and admired its amazing symmetry.
Then it started walking down the rock
and I murmured darkly
This is impossible; shells don't walk.

How dumb can you get? I took the guy
and tossed him back into the sea.
Now you can fly! I said, *And anyway
I didn't like your symmetry.*

    *

Another day we scooped up about twenty
of the little white starfish
with our hands
where they slept half-hidden in the sand
of the shallows
then we put them on a towel to dry
(upside down where they writhed and writhed).
It took them many hours to die.

I use them to decorate my bathroom walls
and I don't know why.

    *

By night with knives and flashlights
we tracked down the tiny blue crabs
who lived in the crevices of the rocks
on the shoreline.

144

Dazzling them with man-light, we pried
and poked into their little homes
and prodded and poked and pried and speared
the things, some of them small as spiders
in our hands.

And though we were not hungry, we ate,
we ate them straight from the fire,
because they were so blue and beautiful
and tasted of the sea
because they were so small and rare.

*

Drop the sails and be silent
There is something here we do not understand

As dark as the receding tides
As delicate as the tiny shrimps who
Tickle their way across my hands

There is nothing to fear in the sea
But ourselves
There is nothing to fear but man

145

Silence Is a Place

Silence is a place inside the lion's eye
where several worlds dissolve
in jungle fever or malaria, and
the seeds of nations never rise

Nowhere is a place within the lion's eye
where many worlds refuse to be, and
mangled nations meet their destiny

I live inside the lion's eye.
Do you know me?

The Lion Tamer

And now, Ladies and Gentlemen, the Star of our Show!

A panther walking *alone* into a cage of three Kanadian
politicians armed with nothing but their wits, a
pre-heated waffle iron and a pack of Rolaids!

or

And now, Ladies and Gentlemen, the Star of our Show!

A Siamese cat walking *alone* into a cage of more or
less ordinary men armed with nothing but electric
shock rods and narcotics!

Who's kidding?

The Blue Hippopotamus

here comes the great river-horse
chewing and mumbling huge blue obscenities
under his breath, taking ten minutes to get
from his shed to the water which is only about
ten yards away, although for him it's ten worlds
(the way he moves)

here comes the great river-horse
taking in everything at a glance:
the zoo, the people, the zebra,
the dumbness of it all, and me

the dumbness of it all, and then
he lowers himself into the hellish pool
(which is too small) displacing tons
of grey water which flop over
the top of the tank extremely slowly, and
whirls the water inside the great tidal hippo waves
which go smush, smush

then the blue hippopotamus is gone
relieved at last of his own great mumbling weight,
having displaced at least ten worlds, one zoo,
one zebra and me

148

The Little Dog

The thing looked like a cross
between a mouse and a box of toothpicks

It had piggy-wiggy eyes and piddled
down the street on more or less legs

Its mouth looked like Jean Harlow's
at the height of her career

I think it had ears
but I can't be sure

It probably lived on vitamins and Geritol,
it wouldn't have survived a confrontation
with a cockroach or a pea

The woman owner looked healthy enough
(probably a cross between good German stock
and hardy British farmers)

Something sensible anyway
to ensure the survival of the species

I wondered if she got it out of a can
called Instant Dog, and added water

I wondered if she got it out of
a freezer in a supermarket
and thawed it out

Ah, for a glimpse of a lean as lightning greyhound
Ah, for a glimpse of animal
neither inbred, cross-bred, silly or shy

I wonder how we got this way

The Demon of Thursday

Thursdays I reserve for going mad
and wondering how the trees grow
(kiss, perhaps, of the living God?)

Thursdays I reserve for being sane
and wondering why some people do not know me
although we have been introduced in dreams

Thursdays, I presume, are for the birds
who pick around for bits of thoughts and grain
inside the garden of my head

Thursdays I reserve for whales
with huge mouths full of plankton
and words I understand too well

Thursdays I reserve for the animals
the angelic and demonic animals
the magic animals more real than real

As the Angels

As the angels and the animals lie
As the saints and leopards sleep
In a huge heap in some forgotten corner
Of the universe
So shall I sleep, O so shall I

Meanwhile I watch as man, O man
That hairless hunter, that gutless wonder
Rides by night in the dark night air
With his floating kidneys
And his ears on fire

I have many secrets
And no particular future

I am surreal and finally here

I am a perfect animal

As the angels and the animals lie
As the saints and leopards go to sleep
So then, so then shall I

Prune

was a huge totally worthless and basically hideous old grey
cat who died

everything dies and I'll get God for that

I might even get God for the manner of this death

because Prune who was grey and hopeless had to
drag half of his paralyzed body across the floor
dripping blood and slime all over
the place

dripping death into his shit-box and keeling over
and lying there

his head resting neatly on his last stool

The Rodeo

Let me ride you, Lord,
Horse of the storms,
Let me ride you out!

You buck and swell
Beneath me, and I swear
I will not fall.

I've ridden the horses
Of heaven. I've been
Through other rodeos than this.

Lord, I think you are a pony.
I've broken beasts
More wild than you.

A Prayer

Thou, be with me now
In the loudest moments of my birth.

The world is out of print.
I have prevailed, but I have not
Identified the earth.

I've tried and died and every song
Returns to plague me
In the loudest moments of my birth.

Hey!—Death comes slow and easy
In the crazy silence of the earth.

But Thou, be with me now
In the loudest moments of my birth.